StoneSoup

Writing and art by kids, for kids

Editor's Note

As I write this, wars are raging around the world. Although a wonderful story or poem can often be a welcome escape, it is also the role of literature to tell the stories that are difficult to tell. In this issue, we open with Part I of a story that explores the terrifying lead-up to the ongoing war in Ukraine through the eyes of a Russian boy growing up there. We'll be publishing Alice Pak's novella *War and Pieces* in three parts over three issues. It is a realistic, moving story, but it's the note of hope it ends on that touches me the most.

When we accepted Palestinian poet Hana Shqairat's poem "Spring Will Revive," the last piece in this issue, little did we know how violently the Israeli-Palestinian conflict would soon reignite. The striving for peace and the thirst for renewal that Hana so poignantly expresses has taken on new meaning now.

We can't know how these conflicts will play out, but we can look forward to the first buds of spring, and we can hope.

D Landolf

Executive Director
Emma Wood

Editor
Diane Landolf

Production Coordinator
Kelly Holler

Typesetter
Jeff Piekarz

Communications
Tayleigh Greene

Blog Editor
Olivia McKeon

Refugee Project
Laura Moran

Director Emeritus
William Rubel

Thank You to Our Donors!

Production and publication of this issue is made possible by our Jane Austen donors ($1,000 and above):

The Allen & Eve Foundation, Sandy & Tom Allen, Anonymous (4), James Evarts, Amanda Fox, Brian Harlan, Gerry Mandel, Brion Sprinsock & Kristine Albrecht, and Sally & Clem Wood.

Cover:
Mountainside Flowers
(Acrylic)
Yanling Lin, 12
Virginia

Stone Soup (ISSN 0094 579X) is published bimonthly, six times per year. Copyright © 2024 by the Children's Art Foundation–Stone Soup Inc., a 501(c)(3) nonprofit organization located in Santa Cruz, California. All rights reserved.

Thirty-five percent of our subscription price is tax-deductible. Consider further supporting *Stone Soup*—visit stonesoup.com/donate.

To request the braille edition of *Stone Soup* from the National Library of Congress, call +1 800-424-8567. To request access to the audio edition via the National Federation of the Blind's NFB-NEWSLINE®, call +1 866-504-7300, or visit Nfbnewsline.org.

StoneSoup
Contents

ART

Flower Crown (iPhone 6)
Alice Pak, 13
Ohio

War and Pieces (Part I)

Misha experiences the first signs of unrest in the Donetsk region of Ukraine

By Alice Pak

This is the first installment of Alice Pak's novella, which we will be publishing over the course of three issues.

Prologue

Misha was the one who showed me a dove for the first time.

It was early spring, that magical time of year when coats and sunshine go hand in hand. Puddles of rainwater were splotched on every street, reflecting every cloud in the bluest blue sky ever like a thousand mirror shards. We were standing by the old swing set on the hill, the one with the rusted rings and peeling red paint. It was a sad little swing, I always thought; someone had built it a decade ago, alone, in the middle of nowhere, and then forgotten all about it. But that was okay. It was *ours*, me and Misha's.

I remember thinking that as I stood up on the swing, swaying back and forth slowly as I gained speed. Misha stood next to me, leaning against the yellow metal poles as he thoughtfully bit into a green apple. I followed his gaze to the crooked, solitary birch tree nearby, the only other thing worth seeing on the hill besides the swing. I could hear a clamor of high-pitched voices bickering somewhere in its feeble limbs.

"Hey, look!" Misha finally spoke, excitedly pointing at one of the highest branches. "Varya, do you see that?"

I squinted, following his finger. On top of the tree, hidden in the vivid leaves, I made out a small white shape. "Is that a white squirrel?"

Misha shook his head. "No. Where have you ever seen a *white squirrel*?"

"I read about those."

Skeptical, Misha decided to ignore my comment.

"That's a dove," he said softly. "A real one. Isn't it pretty?"

I cocked my head, looking up at the figure again. This time I made out a pair of delicate folded wings tucked into the snowy-white feathers, fluttering slightly in the breeze. Two tiny black dots sat above a gray beak, making the dove's expression seem permanently surprised.

"Oh." I shrugged. "Yeah, I see it now."

Misha kept grinning. *Leave it up to him to pay so much attention*, I thought as I glanced in his direction. Sometimes he honestly reminded me of a bird himself: messy jet-black hair, big blue eyes, built a bit too scrawny for an eleven-year-old boy at the time. He didn't look much like me or anyone else in our Ukrainian town of Donetsk, really. I had long blonde hair, amber eyes, and freckles all over my face. No one would ever say that we looked alike, but we felt almost like siblings anyway, growing up together and living in adjacent apartment buildings.

"You know what's cool?" he asked, turning back to me. "Doves are a symbol of peace and freedom, I read. Maybe seeing one is like a good luck charm for us to always be safe and happy."

I rolled my eyes. "That sounds kind of made up. Books aren't always right."

Misha stepped back, mock offended. "How dare you! Books have the answer to everything."

"Where'd you find that?"

"I read it"—Misha sighed—"in a book."

I snorted a laugh, punching him lightly. "All right, all right. Kidding. Let's pretend this is a good-luck charm."

Misha smiled, glancing at the dove one last time before it spread its wings and hopped off the branch, catching the breeze and soaring away. We watched it for a long time as it disappeared into a barely visible pale speck in the sky, flying high among the clouds.

"Ice cream?" Misha suggested, turning to me.

"You bet."

Chapter 1

I guess I could say I noticed something strange going on a long time ago. My blurriest, earliest memories began when I was five and Varya was three.

Our town wasn't strictly Ukrainian or Russian. And I never thought of it as being strictly in either country either; it was almost at the border—somewhere there, in between both lands. Many Russian families such as me and my mom lived there and even more Ukrainian ones did too, and it was completely normal. There were no disagreements or fighting. It always felt like one big family to me, holding each other up and looking out for one another.

Me and my mom loved going on walks at the time. We loved nature. We loved a nice breeze. I mean, we still do, but I guess it got tougher as time passed and events started unfolding.

We were at the local park that beautiful July evening. I always liked the park, honestly. Trees draped in lush greenery towered above delicate benches set deep in the shade; tidy sand pathways created a big loop around a center playground where several swing sets and a slide seemed to bring all the kids out.

I was on the slide, of course. As a five-year-old, a slide to me seemed like an endless, curving road. A rollercoaster. A challenge. A feat only for the bravest souls to take on.

My mom was leaning against the swing set, a small smile playing on her face. I remember the moment captured perfectly in time; strands of her chocolate

I didn't say anything as my mom ushered me into our dark apartment, closing the door behind us and locking all three locks.

brown hair tickling her face, her green eyes lighting up every time I screamed with delight. I even remember her jacket; it was a faded pink color, like curtains in an old lady's apartment.

On my twentieth trip down the slide, my mom suddenly moved away from her spot against the pole, her face hardening. She looked up at the sky and then to some of the buildings on the far side of the park before quickly walking over to me.

"Hey now, Mishka. We got to go," she told me, taking my hand gently.

I pouted. "Can I go down one more time?"

She shook her head. "I'm sorry. We'll come back tomorrow. I promise."

"Pleeeeeease?"

She didn't answer immediately; instead, she pressed a finger to her lips. She seemed to almost freeze, as if listening intently for something.

I tried to quiet my breathing, listening too.

That was when I heard it the first time. The sound that haunted my dreams for the rest of my life.

It was a muffled boom, almost sounding like someone hit a giant metal sheet against a brick wall far, far away. At first I thought it was thunder. A second one followed a minute later, and then a handful of them. I gripped my mom's finger, looking up at her with wide, terrified eyes.

"Mommy, is it going to rain?"

She sighed. "I don't know. But we better get back home."

I silently stumbled after her as she dragged me back three blocks towards our apartment. I didn't say anything as she punched the button for the sixth floor and the elevator flew upward with a small *ding* as a bright "6" flickered onto the screen above the door. I didn't say anything as my mom ushered me into our dark apartment, closing the door behind us and locking all three locks. I didn't say anything up until I finally climbed into bed in my favorite blue Spider Man pajamas and turned on my star-shaped nightlight, which glowed orange and slowly shifted to a yellow and then green and blue and purple until I tore my eyes off and glanced at my mom, who handed me my teddy bear and smiled.

"You sleep well, all right?" she said softly, stroking my hair.

I nodded. "Mommy, why was there thunder today?"

She took a long look out the window, where the sky had settled into a purple-blue twilight dotted with silver stars. When she turned back, she took my hand and squeezed it lightly.

"I'm not sure, Mishka," she whispered. "Don't worry about it, though. Promise me you'll go to sleep once I close the door, okay?"

I snuggled under my blanket. "Okay."

"Goodnight, sweetie."

I remember hearing the door close gently before finally letting the low buzz of motorcycles speeding down the streets pull me to sleep.

Over the next few months my five-year-old brain burrowed those memories deep, deep down, and hearing the strange gunshots slowly became part of my daily life. I suppose I didn't understand it was anything abnormal. I heard them almost every week once it neared twilight, somewhere in the distance or sometimes even seeming closer. My mom always tensed up and led me home in a hurry, so the sounds started being like an alarm of sorts.

A year or two later, I recall walking to school one day when I saw a military jeep zip across the road next to me. It was one of those cars that looked like it had splotches of many shades of olive green all over it like a forest. I looked up at my mom, who was eyeing the disappearing vehicle warily.

"It's a cool car," I said, pulling up the straps of my backpack.

"It's a military car," she told me, which was the first time I'd ever heard that word. "It belongs to the Ukrainian army."

"Why is it here, then?" I asked, puzzled. Avdiivka was never an important town to anyone, let alone the army. The most famous thing here was the Avdiivka Coke Plant, the largest coke producer in Ukraine, which provided us with coal and was the main source of all of our power and heat companies.

My mom didn't respond for a few minutes. Then, she crouched down beside me.

"Listen, Mishka. I want you to understand something," she said, looking into my eyes. "Right now it's not very safe. That is why the army is here; they're trying to figure out what's going on and why we hear strange sounds at night. Promise me you'll be careful, okay? If anything happens to you, anything at all, promise to tell me."

I frowned. "Why is it not safe?"

"I'll tell you when you grow up a little." My mom ruffled my hair gently. "But right now I need to know that you'll come to me about anything."

"I promise." I nodded, smiling at her. My mom's face softened and she smiled back, standing back up and taking my hand the way she always did.

"Well, you better get to school. Come on."

Winter break ended on Jan. 11, which I discovered with a pang of annoyance two nights before the date. I spent nearly all of winter break sledding, playing video games, and hanging out with Varya every second I had available, so when my mom reminded me of my impending fate, I burst into tears.

Once school started, everything became boring and monotonous once more. Classes were held in cold classrooms with even colder teachers that droned on about fractions and conjunctions and states of matter until I found myself watching numbers blink on the clock, waiting for each forty-five minutes to be over. Homework was assigned every day save for Fridays, when the professors would find enough mercy in them to let us off with just some extra work in class.

Every day after school I would come home, eat, and then run off to Varya's

8

The fighting continues in a deadlock near Donetsk and Avdiivka, as Russian separatists and the Ukrainian army clash.

after finishing my homework. Since she was only five at the time, she didn't yet go to school and sat around all day waiting for me to visit her. I'd stay in her apartment for hours, telling her funny stories and describing all the wonders of elementary school while she laughed along. Then once my mom called, I'd bid her goodbye and return home for dinner.

After dinner, my new obsession became tuning the radio and listening to the latest news. It was such an astonishing little thing; a tiny gray box which I kept on top of the dresser that could be turned into a talking-broadcasting machine with just a few turns of the knob. I would play with it every night, extending the metal rod to different lengths and pressing buttons until the static turned to music and sports reporters screaming the latest statistics in soccer matches or tennis.

I loved watching TV. But listening to the radio made me feel like I was a few decades behind, lost somewhere in the 1980s and such, and I loved it.

The night of Jan. 30, after finishing my chicken and rice, I retired to my room as usual and took out my radio, plopping down on the carpet and beginning to tune it in. It always felt so satisfying, listening into the loud, blank static and then hearing it finally start changing frequency, shifting to sounds that would click together into a voice. I flipped through some channels lazily, wondering what to pick. One was a soothing piano playing Chopin. Another was some sort of audio comedy show with horrible artificial laughter that turned on after every sentence said by the characters. A couple of channels down, a man was yelling out commentary over a soccer match in Spain. Next came a church worship group.

I was about to go back and listen to the comedy show until I accidentally clicked the button once more, taking myself to a channel I'd never gone on before. At first I heard nothing; then as I adjusted the volume, I finally began catching snippets of some sort of report being listed off. I turned the volume all the way up, intrigued.

"...the fighting continues in a deadlock near Donetsk and Avdiivka, as Russian separatists and the Ukrainian army clash. It is still unclear whether the situation is being pushed further towards civilian regions, but several reports of gunshots being heard in the area have been received within the last twenty-four hours, meaning the battle is moving closer towards Avdiivka. It is advisable..."

I froze, the radio still in my shaking hands. Then, after a second, I clambered up and ran to the kitchen, where my mom was sitting in front of her computer looking stressed.

"Mom, mom." I tapped her shoulder. "Listen to the radio."

She tore her eyes from the screen and watched as I turned the volume up again and set it down on the table. The news blared through the speakers, every word seeming filled with panic.

"Where did you find this channel, Misha?" My mom looked at me with serious eyes.

"I-I don't know, I was just trying to find something interesting," I stuttered, my eyes wide. "Why is there fighting?"

My mom ignored the question and instead took the radio in her own hands, leaning in to read the few numbers at the top of the channel name. 107.8 FM.

"Is it alright if I hold on to this for now?" my mom said, patting the top of the radio. I shrugged, still uncomfortable. "Yeah. But why did they say there's fighting?" My mom pursed her lips the way she did whenever she didn't want to tell me something.

"I'm not sure," she told me, clapping my shoulder. "But I think it's about time for you to go to sleep, don't you think?"

"I guess." I reluctantly retreated back to my room. Closing the door behind me, I grabbed my pajamas from my shelf and changed into them, leaving my sweater and pants on the stool next to my bed. I climbed into bed, burrowing in my blankets until I felt all warm and snuggled up, before turning off the light switch and pressing the button on my nightlight. Eyes glued to the changing colors, I began counting the number of times I saw the light turn red until I unnoticeably drifted asleep.

I woke up at nine, immediately bolting to the bathroom to brush my teeth. Nine! I was supposed to wake up an hour ago. School started at eight thirty; I'd be so late!

I jogged back to my room and whipped out my uniform, tugging it on as I stumbled into the kitchen to find my mom passed out at the table, her hand still wrapped loosely over a mug of cold coffee. I prodded her shoulder.

"Mom!"

I shook her harder until she finally cracked an eye open and yawned. I stopped.

"Mom!" I said, trying to convey a sense of urgency through my voice, "I'm already late for school! My alarm didn't go off at eight, so I slept for an extra hour! Everyone's probably in math right now!"

My mom sat up and stretched, taking a sip of her overnight coffee and wincing. She glanced at her computer screen, which had turned off while she was asleep, and pressed the "on" button. Nothing happened.

"Ugh," she yawned. "Can't even check the time now. Nine, you say?"

I nodded. "My digital clock wasn't working, so I looked at the old mechanical one on the wall. But I need to hurry! My teachers will be so mad at me."

My mom stood up, still looking tired, flicking the light switch with her finger. Both of us looked up at the ceiling, expecting for the lights to turn on and bathe the kitchen in a golden glow, but the room stayed dark. I frowned.

My mom persistently flipped the switch a couple more times, as if channeling her annoyance into it, but every attempt came as fruitless as the last.

"Why aren't the lights turning on?" I asked, fearful.

My mom shook her head. "Weird. Did the power get cut off at night?"

She slipped her feet into her boots and unlocked the apartment door, stepping out into the sixth-floor lobby. The lights were still out there as well, but our neighbors' door was wide open too, and voices were coming from the living room.

Both of us looked up at the ceiling, expecting for the lights to turn on and bathe the kitchen in a golden glow, but the room stayed dark.

There was no light either, save for what looked to be a half-burnt candle sitting on the table next to a vase of dried roses. We stepped inside, my mom knocking on the door to make our presence known.

A plump middle-aged woman shuffled out of the living room, still in a bathrobe, her pearly white hair in curling rollers. She half-smiled at me and turned to my mom, greeting her hurriedly.

"Come on in, come on in," she said, her speech tinged with a slight Ukrainian accent. "We're all in the living room. Nobody is exactly sure what happened with the electricity."

I shivered. I hadn't noticed until then that it was a couple of dozens of degrees colder in the building than usual, almost as if we were actually outside. The lady clicked her tongue worriedly and pulled a coat out of her closet, wrapping it around me. I thanked her quietly, looking up at my mom, who nodded at me before following our neighbor to the living room.

The room looked a lot like ours: a long gray couch against the wall, on which sat three more people, a round wooden coffee table, and several cabinets along with the TV hung up on the wall. Framed photos dotted one of the walls among pieces of paper with words and doodles which looked like they were made by a little kid my age. I grinned at a drawing of a green bear standing next to a stick figure twice his size, thinking I could easily sketch something better than that.

I turned to look at the people on the couch. They were probably some of the other people that lived on my floor, maybe one of the floors above or below us. One was a middle-aged man with a potbelly covered with a tight-fitting striped tank top who was taking up half the space on the couch. He stroked his thick mustache thoughtfully, looking somewhat angry and sleepy at the same time. Next to him, leaning as far away from him as possible, was a young woman of no more than twenty-five years old. She was clearly the most well-dressed person in the room, sporting a bright pink coat and a matching skirt with a fuzzy hem which took all my willpower to not run up and feel. She was rocking back and forth nervously, fiddling with her gloves as she glanced up at our hostess.

"I'm pretty sure the power is out in the entire area," the third occupant of the room noted. He was also young, dressed in a simple white T-shirt and jeans. He twirled an unlit cigarette in his fingers.

"I believe so," our hostess replied, wrapping herself even tighter in her bathrobe. "Or . . . well, none of the phones are working, at least. I'm assuming something happened to the electricity."

"And the h-heating," the lady in the pink breathed. "I woke up f-feeling like I was sleeping outside in the s-snow."

My mom stiffened up slightly. "Is this because of the battle going on by Donetsk?"

"By Avdiivka, you mean," the young man replied with a sigh. "It's moved closer to us."

The lady in the pink stopped shivering for a second. "Has it?"

The potbellied man sat up with a huff, finally letting go of his mustache. The lady in the pink inched away.

"Unfortunately, yes," he said, his deep voice resonating in the room. "One of the sides probably knocked out the power while they shell each other."

My mom glanced at me with an unreadable expression. I pretended to be interested in the fly on the table.

"What is the fighting over? Land?" she asked.

"Control of the territory," the potbellied man said gruffly. "The separatists are all in for Russia taking the Donbas oblast back so that the anti-Russian terrorists stop shooting at the Russian population, but the Ukrainian military disagrees. They're clashing to see who will have full control over this region."

There was a pause. The lady in the bathrobe let out a cough.

"I'll go prepare some tea."

Everyone watched her leave silently before snapping all eyes back on the man on the couch.

"Why c-can't an agreement be reached? Can't they contact the government for backup instead of trying to s-separate from Ukraine?" the lady in the pink questioned.

"We have tried. The government doesn't have much they can do about it." Potbelly shrugged. "Can't say they care about some small towns on the outskirts. Russia would actually defend us, though. That's why the separatists want to take control of the area."

My mom nodded slowly, looking down at the floor with a calculating gaze.

"Sir, and yourself? Ukrainian native?"

The man boomed a laugh.

"Oh, no," he grinned toothily, "I'm Russian all the way. I moved here 'bout a decade ago to work on the coke plant. Most of the jobs in the incorporation closed down a while back, though, so I've been living off of my savings since then."

The young man holding a cigarette blew his hair out of his face.

"Yeah, the terrorists shot a little too close to the factory," he said, leaning against the wall casually. "They've been doing this for years now, shelling and sending threats."

Both my mom and the lady in pink turned white. "*Threats?*"

He shrugged nonchalantly. "Well, yeah. Saying stuff like, '*Go back to where you came from or else,*' '*Die, Russian scum.*' Most of the terrorists only pelt our area with bullets just cause they hate Russians, you know?"

Our hostess, still in her bathrobe, entered the room again with a sour expression. "No hot water, sadly."

"I guess that got turned off too," he noted. "All of this is so dumb."

"What, having no power?"

"No, the things that are happening," he said, looking up at the ceiling. "The fighting and the terrorism. The disagreements caused by politics."

I didn't understand half the things said that morning. I didn't know what threats were or "politics." I didn't even understand why the power went out for a week and school got canceled; I had to learn about it much, much later.

But I knew something important was happening. Something life-changing, judging from the nights my mom spent up after that, reading and circling newspapers. Judging from the thousands of messages she sent and received for weeks after that. I knew it would change my life, for the worse or for the better.

... to be continued in the May/June 2024 issue of Stone Soup

Dress

By Jaslene Kwack, 13
Illinois

my grandma has a blue cotton dress that she wears at home
it has a different scent every day
the smell of each night's dinner
the breeze from a brisk walk outside
or the dampness of the air during rainy season
the smell of orchids from the florists' shop, pastries from the bakery across the
     street,
freshly cut melon for dessert, steaming morning coffee
the scents of the lotions she uses and her shampoo
stitched deep inside the span of threads within the fabric of her blue dress

her closet is a fusion of attire
eye-catching golf shirts in jolting colors
button-up tops in solid shades
a long, straight dress in sunset plaid
vertical stripes running up and down pastel blouses
she likes modest styles with classy hues
shoes without adornments, elegant traces

there's a Korean proverb, "Clothes are wings"
that means clothes make the person
my grandma says clothes will show
who you are
because people will judge by the first thing they see
how magical it is that we can change how somebody
first interprets us
just by the variation of simple cloth

Annalisa (Acrylic)
By Rebecca Wu, 9
Washington

Growth

A woman gives love and life to a special plant

By Evangeline Gustavson, 10
California

Day 1

Dirt shoved its way into the cracks in her hands, and she watched herself bury the little mound of dirt which supposedly had life. A simple trip to her neighbor's house and here she was. She didn't even bother to ask what type of plant it was, whether she needed to water the seedling constantly or not. She did not even know why she had agreed to care for it. Still, as she buried the seedling, packaged with its own soil, she began to feel a type of hope.

Week 1

The seedling had begun to sprout, and as for the watering, it was even. A little one day, a whole bunch another. It could go a long while as if it were pouring every day, and it could go a long while as if it were in a hot desert. She gave it lots of love. There was resentment too.

Week 2

The sprout flourished into sprouts with the beginnings of flowers. She loved her little plant, for it brought her much joy. Now, though, it grew older and ordered more nutrients. It took up the majority of her life, when there were more important things to be done. Still, they lived on.

Month 1

The plant now measured a foot tall, and its greenness was a sure sign of ultimate health. It now took new responsibilities, like spreading out its leaves wide so it could gather much sunlight. Other days it shriveled them up and shielded them away from the sun. Its growth patterns changed every day. Sometimes it leaned on its wooden support beside it, other times it stood straight up tall. It changed every day.

Month 6

The plant was now almost as tall as the woman who planted it. It was starting to spread out the flower petals beautifully, so that it would attract the bees to come deliver and collect pollen. It swelled with life, and so did the woman. She now put her heart and soul into it; it was her priority now. It was as if the plant was embedded in pure life. It grew all across her yard, and when the night came, it would stretch under a wooden canopy so that it did not get wet from the rain, while its roots soaked in the water. And the woman, who remembered the plant from its seedling days, gave it all it ever needed.

Year 1

The plant now stretched over the entire yard. The neighbors were afraid but at the same time amazed. The very same woman who gave the plant's mother the seeds was surprised to find that it had grown so big. But the plant's mother loved it no matter what, and therefore it grew and grew. It had big responsibilities now too. Its systems worked together, and slowly its flowers evolved into beautiful fruits: reds, oranges, yellows, and greens. It made each one attractive so that the tiny critters of the yard could eat them and spread the fruit's seeds around. It was reaching adulthood, but there was a problem: at this point, it could tell that it would be a short time until it stopped living.

Year 2

The once little plant is dead. One day the woman came into the yard to water and found a dried brown stalk on the ground. She cried and flung the stalk out of the yard. As she collapsed in sorrow, fresh life met her skin. The offspring of the plant comforted her, saying she'd get through this. This is the way of nature; her little plant just went off earlier than usual. Together, they promised. They would get through this together.

Year 3

The woman knows the cycle now. The offspring will be finished in the next year and a half. Steadily, at least. A number of the offspring have already died due to shadows, storms, and other things. None of them are quite as extraordinary as the little plant; they don't grow to a huge size or produce multicolored fruit, but the woman loves them all the same. She wonders how she is still alive after all

continued on p. 19

Mountain (Acrylic)
Kate Fullem, 10
Pennsylvania

this time. Then she reminds herself that her end is coming nearer, and like her beloved little plant, she can sense her end is coming soon.

Year 4

The woman is dead. No one takes her house, for the garden is too wild. As for the offspring, they create offspring and die off. The offsprings' offspring will become older and will eventually die off too, but not without creating their own offspring. They all sense an absence, though, even the oblivious youngsters. Something is off. *The woman doesn't come and swat the bugs off our leaves*, they think. "No," others say, "It isn't that she is not coming. It is that she cannot come."

For the Rest of Time

The woman's spirit floated up and above, through the clouds, up into a golden world above. She has achieved much, and is satisfied. But now she looks around for something. Suddenly he appears. With shaggy brown hair and a happy, glowing face he races toward the woman. The woman shows no surprise to this and races toward the boy in turn. They embrace in the center of the afterlife, having not seen each other in a long time. The little boy is the little plant, except he hasn't always been one. In fact, he never was a plant; he was always a boy, and that was his story.

Strawberry Fields (iPhone 11)
By Natalie Yue, 11
California

Two Poems

By Avery Parsons-Carswell, 8
Florida

Bright Buds

Pink buds as bright
As the sun,
Sprouting like a
Bird hatches,
Tough as warriors

Mirror, Mirror

mirror, mirror
wanting to be
anyone it sees
wanting
to be
the copycat
of you
or me

Rectangular Sky (Canon Rebel)
Madeline Male, 14
Kansas

Valerie Li & the Library of Alexandria

A clever, determined girl builds a time machine and visits the Great Library of Alexandria

By Jubilee Sung, 12
California

Prologue

Some people think I'm brave, but I think everyone is amazing by accident sometimes.

Hi! I'm Valerie Li. I'm 12 years old, and my proudest achievement is making a time machine. I've only made one because my parents got really upset about all the spoons, tape, and tin foil I used and screeched, "Where did our stuff go?"

To be honest, I don't think they liked it when I cried, "To another dimension!" Thankfully I don't care, because I'm shameless!

Chapter 1

"Valerie Mei Li! Come down here right now!" Mom screeches.

Welp, I'm definitely in big trouble—Mom is using my full name. I sheepishly tiptoe out of my room and down the cold wooden stairs, mentally preparing myself for a long, long lecture.

It's been a while, but Mom is still fiery-inferno mad because she has no spoons to eat her Cocoa Puffs. That's why I'm hiding out in my bathroom tub with my cat, Mr. Jiggles, trying to figure out how to make Mom less mad. Really it's her own fault for not providing me with a handy younger sibling to torment. Being an only child is so boring, and it also means I get way too much attention from my parents. I keep telling my parents, "If you give me a sibling, I could annoy him instead of you." But so far, none have appeared.

"Mr. Jiggles," I moan. "What do you think about all of this? It's totally Mom's fault for not getting me a human sibling, right?"

Mr. Jiggles looks at me with supreme indifference, then leaps out of the tub and attempts to eat my shower curtains. He's always been jealous of my curtains because they feature a mountain of dogs and cats taking a bath. He wants to be the only animal in my life.

"No, Mr. Jiggles!" I cry, trying to pry the curtains from his jealous dagger teeth. But it is too late. My beautiful curtain already has a giant, Jiggle-size hole in it. Mom is going to kill me! She's already in a bad mood, and now there's a hole in the bath curtain? Even worse, she'll never believe it was Mr. Jiggles. Soon the noise of our battle will attract her and she'll part me from my iPad forever! Desperate, I frantically try to put the missing curtain piece back, but when the sunlight hits it, I notice it looks eerily like a picture I saw of the Great Lighthouse of Alexandria, torch and all. That's when I get a lightbulb of a crazy idea. What if I try making a time machine again—but this time with the trash my parents were going to toss?

Chapter 2

I quickly stirred my plan to action by making a poster to let my neighbors know I crave their trash. It looks like this:

```
Hi, Neighbors!
GIVE ME YOUR TRASH
I'm Making a Time Machine
(No Moldy Food, Please)
Your Neighbor,
Valerie Li
```

Now I just need to wait to get some trash . . .

Chapter 3

Ding dong, the doorbell is ringing! Someone must have trash! I run downstairs to open the door, but Mom gets there before me.

"Val, why is Mrs. Nolan here? What did you do?" Mom asks, her eyebrows scrunching together like two menacing thunderclouds.

Uh-oh. I guess I need to explain . . .

"Umm . . . I kinda need trash to make a new time machine. I'm sorry, Mom—I just didn't want to take all your spoons and restrict you from eating Cocoa Puffs."

Her eyes soften a bit. She probably realizes if I start making time machines, she might finally have the house to herself again. After all, I'd be in another timeline—running from dinosaurs or something.

"Why didn't you say so? We have a bunch of recyclable trash right here. You didn't need to bother our neighbors. Why, what must they think of us not giving our dear daughter enough trash?"

"Good point, Mom. I'll take my poster off our roof."

"*The roof?* How did you get it there?" Mom exclaims in shock.

"A magician never reveals her secrets!" I cry, rushing upstairs to escape Mom.

From my room, I can hear Mom explaining to Mrs. Nolan I have all the trash I need for ten centuries.

Later today, Dad comes home to a mess of a house.

"What happened here? Why is there trash everywhere?"

"Sorry, Dad! I'm just building a time machine so Mr. Jiggles can visit other worlds . . . and I can go back in time and buy stock in Apple."

"Oh . . . that's nice, honey," Dad says, his nose already buried in his paper. He never really listens, but he'll see. Once I can go to the past, he will be so shocked his eyes will pop out and he won't be able to get distracted ever again. *Muahahahaha!*

Chapter 4

"Finally, it is done! Ladies and gentlemen, marvel at my amazing creation!" I say to no one in particular.

This often happens to me—talking to no one in particular—because there's no one in this house who really listens. I think I even bore Mr. Jiggles, judging by his current fascination with a dust ball.

This is why I am making a time machine. I am bored and need to find an adventure . . . and a way to make money. I am thinking with a pile of money I could buy more cat food to bribe Mr. Jiggles to stay with me so I don't end up alone. They usually say women are afraid to end up alone with cats but personally, I wouldn't mind it. I would love to be a crazy cat woman!

Anyhow, back to my mind-blowing machine—it's finally done! It's mostly made of cardboard but also has some random plastic and paper inside that I found around the house. What I'm looking forward to is proving kids are not as silly as adults think. I will become a child genius! I can do whatever I want and eat so much candy and ice cream my brain will melt!

Anyways, back to reality. It's time to try out my time machine.

"Mr. Jiggles!" I scream. "Come here! It's time to try out the time machine. I'll give you foo-ood!"

"Val, don't be so loud. I'm on a phone call!" Mom screams.

Hmm, I wonder how I learned to scream?

"Okay, Mom. I'll be quiet!"

Mr. Jiggles finally skitters in, probably because he knows who provides his kibbles.

"You made it! Ready to try my time machine?" I ask.

Mr. Jiggles gives me a look that says, *Do I have a choice?*

Holding my breath with excitement, I drop him into my time machine, hope for the best, and tell Mr. Jiggles to pay attention to everything so when he returns, I can journal his experiences.

"Bye!" I shout, my excitement bubbling as I press the red "time travel" button. Ah! To have its smooth red surface finally descending beneath my fingers . . .

Chapter 5

The excitement doesn't last long because not a minute later, I hear an ear-splitting *Meow!* echo from my time machine. My excitement quickly dissolves into terror as I begin to think something terrible has happened. Although I would never admit it, if my sole companion gets devoured by a dinosaur, I just might miss him, but only a bit. Jiggles can be pretty annoying at times. Thankfully, I don't need to think about it, for at that moment, I see a familiar furry head pop out from the time machine.

"Mr. Jiggles! You're back! That was fast. Are you okay?"

To my surprise, he replies in perfect English.

"Are you crazy? I'm your only friend, for goodness sake!"

"Excuse me. I have lots of friends!" I protest, my cheeks reddening with outrage.

"*Suuuuure . . .*" he says. "Whatever helps you sleep at night."

"Wait. Why are you even able to talk? Go back to meowing."

Who knew my cat was so snarky? *Jeez.*

"Well, it's actually your fault. You're the one who stranded me at the Great Library of Alexandria! Why didn't you warn me about the fire? Did you want my fur singed?"

"Wait a second. Did you just say you were meowing around the Great Library of Alexandria? Oo, please tell me you got some cool books!"

"Well actually, you see, I was too busy running for my life to get any books . . ."

What! Is he crazy? He went to THE Great Library of Alexandria and didn't get a souvenir for me? How rude, I pout.

"It's okay, Mr. Jiggles. Let's just go back!"

"What? You want me to return to that hair-singer? Nuh-uh, not happening. Hey, *hey!* Let me go, I am not going back! Let me go!" Mr. Jiggles protests as I snatch my sole companion in my arms and try not to get scratched.

"Don't worry, Mr. Jiggles. We're going pre-fire. Maybe we can save the library . . . 'cause the day it burned, we lost a thousand years of wisdom."

After sprinting into my time machine, I bend down to press the red button and prepare myself to escape this boring old place. I am practically salivating at the thought of doing something heroic (saving the world from itself *and* acquiring some cool new books, a dynamic duo) when a blue light explodes from under my feet and starts to engulf me, spinning me into a tornado of time.

Chapter 6

We land in a glass dome by the sea, in a lush garden filled with bookshelves, fountains, and greenery. Scholars in sandals and flowing togas are lounging in the garden with scrolls in their hands, animatedly discussing the wisdom inside.

From behind a Corinthian column, Mr. Jiggles and I peer at the scene.

"I can't believe I'm actually here," I breathe, wonder lacing my voice. "Did I actually build something that *works*?"

"Please close your mouth. You're drooling on my fur," Mr. Jiggles sniffs.

"*Know thyself*," I whisper, reading the words emblazoned across the main entrance arch. "Wait a second." I goggle. "Shouldn't this be in Ancient Greek or Latin or something? How can I read it?"

"I always told you you underrate yourself." Mr. Jiggles laughs. "Maybe your time machine turned you into a genius."

"Oh, but Valerie Li, you already *are* a genius," says a golden voice.

My dream words. Maybe she'll adopt me?

A beautiful lady with large, intelligent eyes strolls toward us, her humble, cream-color *tribon* flowing from her white shoulders like liquid wind.

"The stars told me you would come, Valerie Li," she says, her musical voice dancing.

"What stars? It's sunny outside!" I blurt.

"Val, stop being an idiot," Mr. Jiggles mutters. "She obviously meant 'at night.' Don't you know who she is? Stop being rude!"

My cheeks redden in outrage.

"Jiggles, why would I know who she is?"

The lady smiles.

"Hypatia," she says, extending a graceful hand to me. "I'm a teacher in this library, which is probably why this cat knows me. I swear I saw you around . . ." Hypatia's face scrunches up in thought for a second. "Oh, I'm sorry. Would you like to talk over a meal? Don't know about you, but I'm famished."

"Uh, sure . . ." I say, still in shock at this strange stranger.

We stroll beneath another dome with cathedral ceilings supported by beautiful golden buttresses and sparkling windows.

"I'll be right back with the morning meal," Hypatia says warmly. "Have a seat anywhere."

A moment later, she breezes back with cone-shaped bread and a bowl full of some kind of shells in sauce.

"What is that?" I ask.

"Oh, these are snails—my favorite! I'm so glad you came on a Tuesday. You just drill a hole in them like this and suck out the meat."

"Umm . . . no thank you."

Hypatia sighs. "Picky eaters."

Mr. Jiggles and I look at each other. I look at the snails again. I am considerably hungry, but . . .

"Do you guys have Cocoa Puffs?" I blurt.

She gives me a look, then proceeds to slurp snails while we nibble on bread, which by the way has sand in it. Then I remember from a history documentary I watched that the Ancient Egyptians used sand to grind their wheat.

"So what is it you wanted to talk to us about?" I ask in between sandy bites.

"Well, I was hoping you could save us. However, the stars are very vague on how."

"Seriously. Of all people, *Valerie*?" Mr. Jiggles gawps.

"*Hey*, what do you mean? I'm *amazing*!" I protest.

"Valerie," Hypatia interrupts. "I'd like to speak with you. Privately, if we may."

"Uh . . . sure."

Hypatia leads me back to the room from whence we came, which is now empty of people.

"Valerie, do you know what our library means?"

"Um, not exactly?"

"For six hundred years, the Library of Alexandria has been a bastion of knowledge. Every time a ship sails into port, we scour it for books, and if we find one worthy of copying, we do. The Bible was first translated into Greek here so that the common people could read it themselves, because we believe everyone should have access to wisdom. As Aristotle said, 'Whether an empire rises or falls depends on the education of its children.' That is why your world is dying."

"How did you know?"

"The stars told me. I saw the destruction of this library, of a thousand years of wisdom, and a world, your world, where the people in power are choosing power and profit over love and wisdom. If you can save this library, maybe you can save your world."

"No pressure!" Mr. Jiggles laughs, sticking his head from around a column.

"This is supposed to be a private conversation!" I huff.

"Pressure can be a privilege, as it means what you're doing matters," Hypatia says, looking at me with eyes as old as time as she slips a roll of parchment into my hands before disappearing into the garden.

Chapter 7

"Do you think she left to get my Cocoa Puffs?" Mr. Jiggles asks.

"You mean *my* Cocoa Puffs?"

"No. I'm hungry too, you know."

"Mr. Jiggles! Snap out of it. We should be thinking about how we can save our world by saving this library!"

"Oh fine. What was that paper she gave you?"

"Oh yeah!" I say, unrolling it.

"*To save the library, you must find the future king. Persuade him the pursuit of power is not the thing.*"

"The future king?"

"C'mon Val, you should know this! Who burns down this library when he burns all the ships in the port?"

"Oh my gosh! Julius Caesar!" I scream. "Uh, how are we supposed to get a meeting with him?"

Mr. Jiggles grinned.

Chapter 8

Everything is set. It's time!

Time? Time for what, you must be wondering. It's time to roll out of a carpet . . . Cleopatra style!

Mr. Jiggles and I did some research and found out Caesar likes women, carpets, and women rolling out of carpets. But only Jiggles will be naked, of course. This is a rated G story.

Hypatia has agreed to present us as a gift. As I am in the rug right now (trying not to sneeze as we cool our heels outside his tent), I must admit, I cannot wait to scare an ancient old man! I wonder if this is how Cleopatra felt.

"Sir, Hypatia says she has a gift from the future for thee," I hear a soldier's muffled voice announce.

"The future?" Caesar asks, looking wearily up from his war maps.

At least I assume the papers I hear rustling are war maps.

"Indeed," Hypatia says, unfurling the gorgeous vermillion carpet we bought for five *debens* at the local souk at his feet. "Two thousand years hence."

"Arghhhhh!" we yell as Jiggles and I tumble forth.

I throw my arms wide, trying to look appealing as Caesar jumps back in shock.

"Hypatia," Caesar chides. "Why dost thou bring me a girl and a cat in a rug?"

"Oh, we heard you like people gifted to you in rugs! You even have a history with them!"

"I'm in history?"

"Yes! You are indeed remembered, but it is a tragic tale of power and betrayal."

"What? But I'm so loved!"

"That is exactly it. Sixty senators are jealous of you, and at this very moment they are conspiring to do you in in a very bloody and personal way. Didn't Spurinna tell you, 'beware the Ides of March'?"

"How did you know? That was a private bull-sacrificing event!"

"It's in a play I read at school."

"I'm in a play? Am I the star?"

"May we stick with the subject here?" I say impatiently. "My point is, please don't burn down the ships in this harbor, as it will burn down the library and the human race will lose a thousand years of wisdom. And for personal reasons, it's not going to help you to become more powerful, as it will just lead to your untimely and very painful death."

"You've got to choose love over power, friend," Hypatia says gently. "You're already the most powerful person in the empire. When will it be enough?"

"I do have trouble sleeping," Caesar says. "I think I'm a little stressed constantly having to conquer all these countries."

"When I'm stressed, I eat Cocoa Puffs," Mr. Jiggles offers helpfully, holding out a plastic baggie.

"You had a stash all this time?" I ask, and Mr. Jiggles and Hypatia hush me.

Caesar looks thoughtful.

"Yes, perhaps I shall try these so-called Cocoa Puffs. Thank you for your suggestion. Perhaps I shall not set fire to the harbor's ships after all . . . maybe I should hang out with my Cleo more."

"I think we just gave him a free therapy session," I whisper to Mr. Jiggles. "Maybe I've found my calling!"

"I think you need to finish sixth grade first." Mr. Jiggles laughs.

Chapter 9

As Jiggles and I stand by my time machine with Hypatia blowing kisses at us in farewell, I start to wonder what my world will be like now that we've saved it. Will there be flying cars? No wars? No global warming?

Although I am sad to leave, I cannot wait to see my new and better world. Hopefully, I did not erase my birth. But I guess that's a small price to pay when you've just saved the world.

Game of Peekaboo (Nikon COOLPIX L830)
Hannah Parker, 13
Vermont

Lighthouse and I

By Aiden Zhang, 8
Virginia

I gleamed across the ocean,
As I stood up on the lighthouse.
Before I realized anything,
A light shined on me.
The sound of waves
Scared me
I had to rush inside.
As usual,
I purred.

Astrophe

A cat tries to avoid a trip to a fearful place

By Giles Trim, 9
England

I was having a lovely nap on the Flat-Bit-Where-The-Warm-Stuff-Shines when I smelled the dreaded cage of Strange Moving Enclosures and Sharp-Things-With-Wet-Stuff-in-Them-Handled-by-Tall-Tail-lesses-in-White.

No. Don't go down the Up-Down-Boxes. Don't. The Tall Tail-lesses were trying to bring me to the Bad-News-Place. And I hated that terrible place. It had visited me in bad dreams many times. My friend in the next Big-Hard-Walls-With-See-Through-Bits had told me of it. He had described it as "a terrible place, where there are many other cats and many Tall Tail-lesses." But then I smelt my food and heard it being scooped into a bowl. Did I want the food even though I smelt my cage? Or would I just stay up here? I decided to investigate. I jumped to my feet and went down the Up-Down-Boxes.

As I reached the end of the Up-Down-Boxes, I saw the food holder was in the cage. Then, as I was approaching the food holder, hoping to drag it out, the Tall Tail-lesses leaped out from behind me! I started to run back up the Up-Down-Boxes as fast as I could. But they were already behind me and making chase.

Wow, they are really fast! I thought. I ran and ran. Sometimes I ducked under them, but they were always behind me! I ran up and down, left and right, but they were very insistent with their chasing. I heard the cage door rattling. Suddenly, the cage was in front of me. I stopped instantly ... but they had me cornered.

These weird Tall Tail-lesses! Why can't they just understand what I say to them? I ask for food, they brush me. I tell them I'm thirsty, they pat me. And now, they were trying to put me in the Dreaded-Cage-of-Strange-Moving-Enclosures-and-Sharp-Things-With-Wet-Stuff-in-Them-Handled-by-Tall-Tail-lesses-in-White! The taller of the two was making noises, but I couldn't understand them. *Why do they do that?*

As the shorter Tall Tail-less grabbed me round the middle I growled: "No thank you. I would rather sleep on the Big-Soft-White!" The shorter one almost dropped me. Both Tall Tail-lesses looked at me, silent, their mouths open wide. After a long moment of silence, the taller one made a funny noise like "soh ree."

Then they picked me up gently, carried me up the Up-Down-Boxes, and put me carefully on the Big-Soft-White. What strange creatures they are!

Morning. Sunset. Night.

By Kai-Yi Olsen, 6
Tennessee

The Morning is here and the children all let out a cheer.

The Sunset said goodbye. He yawned.

The children said good night.

It's dark and scary.

But I am brave.

Drop after drop we look outside.

Nothing comes back.

Feathers (Watercolor)
Victoria Gong, 11
New York

I Don't Want to Run

Bird-watching helps Dante find peace after the death of his grandfather

By Dante Chowla-Song, 11
New York

The freezing wind howled past me like a ferocious wolf, biting at my toes and fingers. A foul smell arose from the deep black garbage bags, stockpiled messily on the sidewalk. The buildings looked like metal bars, imprisoning me inside my own mind. This was New York City, not a good place to grieve or endure loneliness.

The past few weeks had been weeks of sorrow for my family. My grandfather had just died and it hit all of us hard. My grandfather had died after stumbling on a treadmill. He had already been struggling with diabetes and heart problems, but none of us anticipated for him to pass this soon. At the time of the accident, my grandfather was living in California so none of my immediate family saw him before he died. The funeral had been especially tough for me.

At the time of the funeral, I did not know my grandfather very well. My family didn't visit California very often, maybe once every two years. I was nine, so that meant I had been with him only four times in my life.

At the funeral, everyone was crying. I didn't know how to feel. I was young, and this was the first major loss I had experienced. I had never attended a funeral before. The walls were lined with pink and purple flowers and the priest gave a homily for a long time. I was bewildered. What were all the crazy words he was saying, such as "congregation" and "resurrection"? What was that long red-and-black cloak he was wearing? I did not understand his job. When the pallbearers carried the casket with my grandfather's body in it, I was too frightened to look at his dead upper body. My mom said, "You don't have to look at the body. It's okay." I felt guilty anyway. I remember thinking afterwards, *I should have gone up and given my final regards to him.* After the services, the remainder of the funeral was a blur to me.

This was the second weekend after his death and we were all still in mourning. The absence of his cheerful presence every time we called was evident. We were sauntering to Central Park on a cold autumn day. I had brought my binoculars and had decided to go bird-watching. I had been bird-watching for around a year, so I had gotten used to going every so often. I had my head down, trying not to think back to the funeral when a voice interrupted my blank state of mind.

"Are you okay, Dante?" my mom asked worriedly.

"I'm fine," I replied in a dull voice.

"Okaaaay," my mom commented while raising an eyebrow. "If there's anything you need to talk about, I'm here," my mom stated. The sidewalk felt stiff on my feet and my heavy clothing held me down to the ground. The sky matched my downcast mood and was gray and gloomy. I was pushing my way toward the 90th Street entrance to Central Park. Just a few more blocks in the heavy wind until I arrived in Central Park.

The second I stepped into Central Park, everything abruptly changed. The giant brick skyscrapers were replaced with bright cherry blossom trees and the garbage smell became a warm earthy scent.

"We're here!" I enthusiastically remarked. "Where do we go now?" I asked.

"Well the best place to go bird-watching is in the Ramble, so let's start walking southwest from here," my dad replied. We started strolling toward the Ramble, and I had the chance to appreciate all the plants and nature. There were spider plants, with their bright green-and-white leaves sprawled in all directions. Striking red, blue, pink, and purple flowers blooming in the spring. Towering red oak trees with their bright scarlet leaves. I loved the way the red, green, and yellow colors blended together. There were too many brilliant plants and colors to count. I also observed many different animals. There were squirrels scavenging for nuts. Sparrows seeking seeds under the benches. I felt my chest widen with all the beautiful animals and plants, all thriving in Central Park. The stroll to the Ramble took about twenty minutes, but it seemed all too fast with my eyes darting this way and that, taking in all of Central Park's nature.

I barely noticed the sign that my family had arrived at the Ramble until my dad declared, "We're here!"

"Already?" I asked, astonished.

"Yes, look at the sign in front of us," my dad replied. I took a glance at the sign and it read, "The Ramble" and was followed by a map. We walked along a rough dirt path into the Ramble and experienced another change in scenery. The trees became denser and their translucent leaves allowed little light on the ground. There were more lush bushes and the path was now completely soil. We went down a dust trail until we reached further into the Ramble. A stream trickled as we walked across the bridge over it. It was a small stream but flowing fast as it rushed and glided downhill. The chirping of birds intensified as we got closer to the center of the Ramble, but we were yet to see our first rare bird. We kept listening and gazing around for bird signs, trying to spot a rare bird. The trees and bushes all seemed still and silent around us, like time was frozen except for the plodding of our feet and the running of a nearby stream. After a few minutes of restless glancing and pacing I sensed movement in a spindly young tree next to us. I focused on the tree for several seconds before I saw a dash of red as a brilliant male cardinal showed itself.

The cardinal was striking red. Its lizard head had a dash of white and its tail also had a hint of black. It flitted in and out of the treetops, showing itself here and there. Then, a few seconds later another cardinal appeared. This one was female with brown and beige feathers. Suddenly I realized, the male cardinal had been chasing after the female the whole time! The male cardinal flared its feathers in an attempt to draw the attention of the female. Its feathers were a deep, beautiful cherry color in contrast to the cardinal's deep-black face. I held out my hand with bird seed for them. They seemed hesitant at first, but after a few long minutes they realized I wasn't a threat. The male cardinal was bolder and was the first bird to fly to my hand. Its little black feet tickled my bare hand. "Hee ha ha," I couldn't help but giggle softly. The male cardinal grabbed a seed and immediately flew away. The female cardinal followed the male's lead and jumped onto my hand. It also tentatively took a seed and flew off. After that encounter, the male and female cardinals flew off together.

I held out my palm with bird seed, and soon warblers, thrushes, and sparrows all flew to my hand. There was no stopping the birds coming and going from my palm. I had to refill my hand several times, and eventually, the birds got bored of my bird seeds and flew off. My family and I walked around the Ramble for a few minutes, just taking in the woodland nature and red and yellow falling leaves. The walk around the Ramble was relaxing and calming. We saw Barry the Owl, a year-round resident of Central Park, and many other animals such as chipmunks and squirrels.

After a while of bad luck for spotting birds, I finally spotted a red-tailed hawk. It was sitting dead still in a tree, its watchful eyes observing the scene below. It was mostly brown, with dark red in its tail. It was hard to see against the brown trunk and branches. I used my binoculars to get a better look and saw that the hawk never blinked. I learned later that hawks have three eyelids. Their third eyelid moves horizontally to clean the eye, and they never close their eyes completely.

Suddenly, it swooped to a nearby tree in an attempt to catch a squirrel. I missed its first dive, and then it dove a few more times. The attempts were futile. The squirrel had escaped into a hole in the tree.

It was magnificent to gaze at the hawk's giant wingspan and the way it dove with its claws out. Its beak gleamed in the sunlight and looked dangerously sharp. After the swing and miss with the squirrel, the hawk glided off in the wind.

After thirty minutes of walking around aimlessly, I got sleepy. I sat under a canopy of red and crimson leaves to rest my exhausted eyes and legs. I leaned my back against the sturdy trunk of a nearby tree. I ran through many thoughts in my mind and pushed away the thoughts about my grandfather. I had to face them eventually, though. His smiling face kept coming up in my mind. I finally acknowledged that I had to think about him and his life.

He was a generous grandfather, giving me presents every year, and was always kind to me when I visited him. My family would FaceTime him often, so we could catch up and check in. The last time I saw him was when my family took a walk by the riverside with him. It was a delightful crisp day and you could smell the fresh sea and feel the mist on your face. My parents had bought my sister and me ice cream and we walked as we licked our giant scoops of iced dessert. It was a pleasant walk and we had caught up on things with my grandfather, like what has been going on in California, and how he's doing. I asked him what he was watching on TV. He replied, "I don't watch TV except for the news. It just isn't interesting to me now." I was confused. How could you outgrow TV? I had so many questions for him. I understand now that entertainment isn't everything. My grandfather would always sit down with me and explain how in the old days, they never had computers or phones and they had to find other ways to have fun. He would show me the dusty old books he used to read and teach me about the past. When it was time to leave, I was sorry to say goodbye.

My grandmother and grandfather were divorced, and my grandfather had remarried. He had married a woman named Catherine, and Catherine didn't like my grandma very much. Catherine was a small agreeable woman and my family had no problem with her. I never saw my grandmother and grandfather together for this reason.

As I was thinking about my grandpa and his life, I began thinking the same question again and again. *What would he have wanted for me?*

I knew the answer.

I knew he would have wanted me to live a long and happy life and to not dwell on his absence. He would have wanted me to move on and accept that he had passed away. I had never really accepted the fact that he had died. In the back of my mind I still expected to see him the next time I went to California. I had been caught up in the fast-moving tide of life and hadn't had any time to think about him. Right then I made a decision.

I would not let his death stop me from enjoying life.

I would remember him for who he was to me and grieve him, but I would never let the dark hole in my chest swallow me up in remorse and sorrow.

I realized that this whole time I had been running.

Running away from his death and his passing.

But I was tired.

Tired of running from the inevitable. If I had ignored his death for the rest of my life, I would have always been burdened.

On the walk home, suddenly the trees seemed a bit greener, the sky seemed a bit lighter, everything felt a bit more beautiful. It felt as if a giant weight had been lifted from my back and swept off in the wind. I started asking my parents questions about my grandfather, wanting to know more about him. "Where did he live in his childhood? What was his job? Where did he work?" I wanted to know everything about him. It felt as if the dark hole in my chest had closed up and the world felt less heavy. I knew I had to live life out to the fullest extent. The world sped up as I walked home, and now I thought more about life and all the beautiful things. The smallest smile, the feeling of waking up, wearing my favorite sweater all felt sweeter and fuller to me.

In some ways I was a bit more timid but never let up on the thrill and excitement.

I was more thoughtful, thinking more about the smallest things and my decisions. I was less rash and more reflective of myself.

I never forgot the lessons my grandfather passed on to me through his death.

Live freely, courageously, and vitally in spite of awareness of death.

Everything is temporary.

Live life to the fullest.

Don't run from death.

You Remember

The second-person protagonist pieces together memories of a life

By Beatrix Mackil, 13
New York

You know that you're falling before you open your eyes. You are plummeting rapidly through the darkness. Nothing is around you but pure blackness, uninterrupted by color or light. You try to scream in a panic, but you can't tell if any sound came out. The silence is too loud. You want to sit up, to grab onto something solid, but your arms are pinned to your body and you can't move. Struggle is pointless, you realize as you continue to fall. There is nothing, there never was and never will be anything at all other than the darkness. You feel numb, like every piece of you is slowly fading away. You disappear into the darkness, you succumb and let it wash over you, lulling you to sleep.

You open your eyes. Blue, blue, blueness fills your view, and the light is so bright that you're blinded temporarily. Blinking, you realize that it's the clear, open sky you see above you, smooth and unblemished like a perfect china bowl. Groggily, you reach up to touch it, expecting it to feel cool and smooth. But nothing is there. Aching, you sit up, every part of you feeling like it weighs more than an anvil. As you shakily stand, a wave of heat surrounds you and the air almost bubbles as it meets your skin. Your mouth feels so dry, like it's coated in sand. *Water*, every part of you is begging. *Water, water, water.*

You stumble forward and look around. Dry, sun-parched grass sticks up from the ground in dangerous spikes, a menacing shade of yellow. A wide, boundless expanse of sky meets the flaxen grass on the horizon. Everything is flat except for a few buildings, far in the distance. Gray and plain, they cling to the earth like hunched, weeping figures, crumbling around the edges. You know you need to get to the buildings, get water, and figure out where you might be. Have you ever seen those buildings before? You reach into the recesses of your mind, but all you find is a great blankness, like an empty room swept bare. Only this most primal need for hydration moves you along. You continue toward the house, its mild destitution appearing to you like a palace if it contains the thing you seek. The buildings are easily a mile away, however, and you're unsure if you'll make it that far. Head throbbing and throat burning, you feel exhausted. Continuing on is futile.

You fall to your knees, the sharp grass pricking your hands. You close your eyes, but respite does not come.

You are in a lovely garden, full of beds bursting with beautiful flowers. Birds sing from fruit-speckled, velvety treetops, providing a canopy of shade over the soft blue daybed on which you recline. Spreading out around you is lush green grass, soft and inviting. A little girl, clearly no more than seven or eight, with long, flowing dark curls dances around, her soft white dress billowing out around her as she spins. She giggles and smiles at you, her deep brown, sparkling eyes trusting and warm. She holds out a hand to you, and you take it, the little fingers wrapping around your palm. Pulling you up, she spins you around the garden. "Dance with me! Dance with me!" You laugh and spin her around, and she twirls and twirls, free as a bluebird, until she collapses into the grass, still laughing. You lie down beside her, and she rolls onto her back. Her fingers are still intertwined with yours. Together you look up at the trees and the summer sky. Her head nestles into your shoulder, her silky hair tickling your ear. "I love you, Papa." You don't respond, just squeeze her hand.

You start awake, your breathing hard and jagged. You pant for air, and then choke as you remember how hot it is. Your mind races, rushing to catch up with everything you saw. That girl in the garden, her name is Calliope. Calliope, your daughter. Where is she? You suddenly recognize an ache in your heart that you never realized had been there the whole time. You miss this child with the wild, beautiful spirit. You love her more than anything. You need to find her.

Frantically you scurry to your feet, ignoring the sharp, hot flashes of pain that shoot through your legs, and you run. Racing, stumbling, and racing again. Your eyes squeezed shut, you feel the sticky air rushing through your ears. Suddenly you trip over a thick wooden beam. You snap your eyes open and see the porch steps beneath your feet, rough wood peeking through the worn whitewash. Seeing this rubs away at something in your mind. Something itches in your thoughts, but you can't tell what. Your eyes shut again in concentration.

You are holding a box made of elegant, glossy blond wood. A small, delicate latch holds the lid flush with the base, every carved detail displaying peerless craftsmanship. You are standing on the shoreline of a beach, feeling cold waves calmly lapping against your feet. Grits of white sand and pieces of broken seashells float to your ankles, softly drifting through the tide. But the stronger feeling that is coursing through you is writhing apprehension. You feel like electricity is coursing through your veins, and you swallow hard to fight the wave of nausea that sits in your stomach. *Focus*, you think to yourself. You ignore your shaking hands and instead run over your words that have been writing themselves in your heart for months.

You hear a noise behind you, and you quickly slip the box into your satchel. You turn around and see a woman dressed in a long, silky blue dress. Her dark curls are braided and wound into a loose twist at the nape of her neck. In the dim twilight, her brown eyes seem to glow with warmth. She slips out of a tall wrought-iron gate covered in vines and carefully closes it behind her. "Camille," you call to her, hoping she does not notice the tremor in your voice. When she smiles at you, the corners of her eyes curve like two halves of a heart. She walks down the beach towards you, her skirt waving and flowing gracefully as she moves. Wordlessly, she slips her hand into yours. She looks into your eyes, like she's searching there for something she's lost. "It's a lovely sunset," she murmurs, looking out again into the rosy glow fading into the cool blue dusk. Your heart pounds as you gently pull back your hand. For a moment she looks hurt and lost, until you pull out your box. She claps her hands over her mouth, and pearly tears well up in her eyes, which smile even more than before.

Camille, Camille, Camille, you whisper, in time with your heartbeat. As the stark, dusty porch comes back into focus, so do your memories. You remember this beautiful woman, gentle and kind, and your spirited, clever little girl. You recall the bower on the shore where you built your home together, surrounded by gracefully curving birches. You remember how much you love them both. You squeeze your eyes closed as hard as you can. You need to see them again, you need to remember more.

But this time, you're in a large room lined with plush red velvet. Magnificent arched windows keep out a steady downpour of rain, accompanied by deep, rumbling thunder that shakes the whole house. A tall man in a rumpled gray suit stands by the window, peering out and stroking his immaculate mustache. "Typical for Paris at this time of year," he grumbles, shaking his head.

You feel a shiver go down your spine as the house shivers with each blast of thunder. "Papa," you ask, your childlike voice quavering, "why must the thunder be so angry?"

The man turns to you and kneels down. "Angry? No, no. The storm is magnificent, strong and mighty and beautiful. He scoops you up in his strong arms and holds you up to the glass. "See how it shakes the trees with only a breath of wind? See how it pours down water onto the plants, giving them life? Look how powerful and lovely the storm is." You nestle into his coat. It smells like pipe smoke and old books. In the circle of his arms, you are protected from anything. He says the storm is beautiful, but you'd rather be here, just in case. He looks you in the eye. "You have a storm inside you, Andre. I cannot wait to see the magnificent things you do." He smiles at you, and his gray eyes shine like two pools of moonlight. "Now, how about a story? Yes?" You smile, nodding excitedly. He puts you down on a soft plush armchair that smells just like his shirt. He walks over to a wall of bookshelves on the far side of the room. He mutters and shakes his head with mock seriousness, stroking his mustache. Then he pulls out an old green leather-bound volume from the far left, its gilt-edged pages promising many splendid tales inside. He inspects it for a moment, then shakes his head. "No, I don't think so . . ." You bounce on the seat, impatient, swinging your legs a foot above the soft carpet.

Then a door gently opens, and a slender woman with artfully coiled flaxen hair walks in, holding a tray of beautiful blue china cups, shining and perfect like the sky on a summer day. *They match her eyes*, you think whimsically. She laughs, the sound bell-like, tinkling like high keys on a piano. She sets down the tray and slips an arm around the waist of your father. "Stop torturing the poor child, Valentin. He seems ready to spring off the seat!" He turns around and kisses her cheek, and she slips the book out of his hand, inspecting the title. "Ah . . . *Le Petit Prince*," she reads off of the cover. "You're in for a treat, mon cheri, if your father will ever read it!"

With a deep laugh echoing the booming thunder outside, your father walks across the room in two long strides and sinks down into the chair, scooping you into his lap. His slight beard tickles the top of your head. "Mama! You come too!" You call gleefully. She smiles and perches on the armrest of the chair, leaning into your father's shoulder. "Now start, Papa, read!" He sighs and opens the book, flipping through the foreword. Snuggled tight into the soft chair, with Mama and Papa around you, the thunder seems less loud, and the rain pours less violently than before. Papa clears his throat, and with the steady drum of raindrops and the crackle of the fire in the background, he begins.

You know who you are. You know, you know, you know. You were a boy once, hiding from thunder in your papa's coat, listening to your beautiful mama's musical laugh. You were a man on a beach, proposing to a woman named Camille, whom you loved more than anything, until you were a father and there was a child named Calliope who took your whole heart. Your name is Andre Moreau. You were a husband, a son, a father, a man who loved more deeply than words can explain. And you will love again. You will get back to them. You don't know where you are, but you now know who you are, and that's all you need.

But it isn't quite all you need. You are still so thirsty. You stumble up the bare stairs, and they creak with every step, like trees bending in a storm. You reach for the cold metal knob on the plain door, grasping it firmly and turning it. You push open the door, and step into the cool, dark house. As your eyes adjust to the dim light, you take in a small room, empty and spotlessly clean, with whitewashed walls and a neatly swept floor. The baseboards are scuffed and the single overhead lamp is quite dim. "Hello?" you call, not sure if you want anyone to answer. You hear a noise, a shuffling from deep inside the house. A door creaks open slowly, and an ancient woman emerges. She is hunched over an elaborately carved wooden cane with a gold top, and she is wearing a vast black dress, pearl buttons dotting the bodice like shining stars in the broad night sky. She has a pale silk scarf flowing over her arms, like a stream of pure moonlight. Her face is deeply creased and wrinkled, all of it giving an impression of belonging to another time altogether, except for her clear, bright eyes, which are wide open. Her hair is silvery-white, and coiled atop her head like a nestling dove. "Who is there? Who is there?" she calls, her voice low and creaking just like her home.

"I mean no harm," you answer. "I've been traveling and I'm quite thirsty. Would you mind if I stayed for a minute to have some water and rest? I'll be on my way in no time at all."

She looks you up and down, then purses her lips. "That will be fine. Come this way."

She sweeps out of the room, and you hurry after her. You follow her into a kitchen that is all in white. The old cookstove, the cupboard, the table are all perfectly clean and white, like snow had just fallen in the home alone. The one black object is a large water pump in a corner. The woman lifts a tin mug out of a drawer and fills it at the pump, sighing with labor. She wipes down the already spotless table and sets down the water before you. Eyes wide, you snatch the vessel and drink viciously, lapping up the water like a dog. Only after you feel the last of the ice-cold liquid pour down your throat do you wipe off your mouth and thank the woman effusively. She just shakes her head and makes some odd sort of muttering sounds. She begins pulling out strange things from the cabinets: colored glass bottles that shine like jewels, lumpy paper packages, and carved wooden boxes. She moves around the little space like a bird collecting soft bits for her nest. For such an aged woman, she flutters around the space.

"So," she begins with her back to you, "What is your name?"

Mechanically you answer, "Andre Moreau, ma'am."

She whisks around to you abruptly, her fine brows creasing together into a single furrowed line. "What are you *doing* here?" she murmurs, almost to herself, but you think it impolite not to answer.

"I'm looking for my family and my home. My wife, Camille, and my daughter, Calliope. They share my surname. Do you know of any of them?" The woman gets a very strange, unreadable look on her face. She shivers in an unconscious way, and edges away from you. Then she closes her eyes and inhales deeply, her wrinkled hands clutching the table behind her, like she is afraid that she might fall. "Ma'am, are you all right? Can I help you?"

The woman mutters to herself, shakes her head sharply, and opens her eyes. "I . . . I think you'd better go out back," she says gently, gesturing towards the door. Warily, you cross the room and push open the door with a heave. A wave of sizzling heat nearly pushes you back into the house, but instead you step forward, squinting against the suddenly bright light. You make out the shape of a wide, low tree stretching its branches over the sun-cracked land. As your eyes adjust to the light, you see the ground is scattered with many large rocks.

No, you think. *Not rocks.*

Tombstones.

You feel something inside of you plummet. Your heart skips a beat, and then continues pumping twice as fast. Panic rises inside of you and you begin to shake. You turn back to the woman, who is still hovering in the dark doorway, her face in her scarf. Trembling, you kneel down on the hard ground and brush some soil and dust off of the surface of the first terrible stone.

```
Valentin Moreau, 1832-1908, and Elise Moreau, 1843-
1908. Loving husband and wife.
```

Your eyes widen in horror. *Papa! Mama!* Frantically you grope at the next.

```
Camille Durand-Moreau, 1858-1936
```

```
Calliope Moreau, 1897-1959
```

A horrible sob rises in your chest. A terrible darkness wraps its tendrils around you. You scream, shaking and pounding the dirt with your fists. As you yell, all fight, all life leaves you. You are silent and perfectly still. So is the rest of the world. Everything is gone. Your heart has been wrenched away. You do not feel anything. You are numb and cold. Slowly, mechanically, you crawl to the last stone and read the writing.

```
Andre Moreau, 1849-1934.
Beloved son, husband, and father. May he rest in peace.
```

Memory Rock

By Clarie Pierce, 10
Maine

I am the memory rock,
I will keep your memories safe.
I've been here for ages,
I am a special place.

Here's a list of things I've heard,
things I've seen,
a few thoughts, and one request.

The things I've heard,
the things I've heard!
I've heard the seagulls . . .

talk, talk, talk.
But my favorite song is . . .
the song of the tide
in
out,
in
out,
in
out.

The things I've seen
oh, what I've seen.
I've seen "I do's" and
the happiest kid play.
As the sun sets
I watch a picnic
and a hermit crab play.

But come close . . .
let me tell you my favorite part.
It's at night when the sun sets and says
good night,
just for the moon to say hello.

Now this beach is my home,
it's a lovely home,
and I'm not the only resident.
This is a home to thousands of creatures
both big and small.
Some in the depths of the ocean
and some on top of me.

You see, I am the memory rock
so come see me and make a memory,
I will keep your memory safe.

Electric (iPhone 11)
Natalie Yue, 11
California

Three Poems

Iris Chalfen, 11
United Kingdom

Papa

"Papa, why do you look so stern?"
"Hannah—"
"I just want this to turn—"
"We can't have this conversation this much."
My father pulls away at my gentle touch.

At this, salty pools in my eyes begin to leak,
I suddenly feel shy and meek.
I turn my back and run outside.
I run for somewhere else to hide.
I run through my secret hedge tunnel,
run so fast I almost stumble.

Coming to the wood shed-house,
I crawl to the corner like a tiny field mouse.
I hug my knees, let the rivers run down my cheek,
there's a cut on my knee,
I don't care, I don't speak.

But my mind is racing:
Why, why why is he so sad?
What is so bad?
Is all this because of me?
Or does everyone feel like a chopped down tree?

Southwold

(Stare the large window.)
I stare out of the large window frosted in sunlight. The seagulls debate early in the morning, flying high over the tipped-up roofs.
(Sunlight-seagulls debate in morning.)

(High the tipped-up roofs.)
My ears open, letting in the rushing sound of crashing, golden waves. I imagine them smacking themselves against the rocks.
(Open letting in sound.)

(Them smacking against.)
One by one each bubbling valley opening to a crash of white thunder, stretching out across the crawling sand, licking up pebbles before dragging them back under the sea.
(Up pebbles.)

Stare the large window.

Untitled

Blue sky
Yellow sun
Trees green
Packing done
House is quiet
Quiet still
The only sound
Is fridge
Drill drill
Owl watches
Spinning chair
Spikey brush
Tangled hair

Betta Fish (Colored pencil)
Claire Cui, 11
California

Elena's Scarf

Siyona's family ends a memorable trip to San Sebastian with a delicious Basque meal.

By Siyona Agarwal, 11
Massachusetts

I waved my hands back and forth, waiting for my ruby red nail polish to dry. My mom hurried around the house looking for a hairbrush. "I'll wait outside," my dad yelled, grabbing the apartment keys. I ran into the bathroom and frantically brushed my hair and sprayed detangler. I climbed down two steps at a time and burst outside into the San Sebastian daylight. We waited for our wonderful hosts, Inaki and his family, who were natives of San Sebastian and had become good friends. They were picking us up to go to a restaurant located in a small village about twenty minutes away from town. Our friends had raved about the restaurant, and I was really looking forward to having a good meal after a whole day of being a dolphin—swimming, surfing, swimming!

It was hot and humid outside, and the air was hanging on me. I worried that sweat beads forming on my back might soon turn into a waterfall and soak my pink cotton dress. We took a quick selfie, and I was grateful that our friends arrived soon. We hurried inside the car. We parked and walked to the restaurant. As we entered, I felt a cold wave and greeted it with a smile. After a minute, my arms were lined with goosebumps and my mom said, "Wow! Look at you. You're like a little strawberry!"

All the adults had to get the tasting menu, because we were a group of more than six people: Marta, Mikel, their parents Inaki and Elena, and my parents. I felt grown up, as I was allowed to order á la carte from the adults' menu. I considered the menu and decided on grilled steak and vegetables.

"Have the apple pie. It's wonderful," Inaki told me.

"Yes!" Marta agreed. "I'm going to change mine to apple pie too."

As the server poured wine for the adults, Elena noticed that Marta was shivering and offered to get the jacket she had forgotten in the car. "I'm okay," Marta said, rubbing her bare arms. The parents sipped on wine while Marta looked up to see if she was sitting underneath the AC vent. Were my goosebumps from cold or excitement? Perhaps both! Slowly and hesitatingly, Elena pulled a scarf from her purse and gave it to Marta, but not without a worried look. "Don't get it dirty. This is my favorite scarf," she said. It was thin, silky, and white with dark red and green spots. Marta was known for being a messy eater while Elena was very careful.

I started the first course of olives drenched in a dark green puree by slurping the puree and saving the olives to savor at the end. "Try the olive, it's magical," Elena said. The olive burst and melted away the moment I put it in my mouth. I realized that the olives were made of white chocolate.

I looked down to see a black ball appear on my plate. The server started explaining. The moment he said, "squid ink," Marta pulled the scarf back with concern. The slippery eel and caramelized apples kept escaping my fork as I tried to lift them up to my mouth.

Everybody moved on to their many main courses, while I got my steak. Four strips of pinkish red surrounded by crispy brown edges. On the side was a small blue pot the size of my palm with carrots, mushrooms, and other vegetables. The tender, juicy steak was gone in no time. I felt kind of full, but I really wanted to try the pigeon, which was the last course on the tasting menu. While everyone else worked through their courses, I admired the wooden twisted sculpture on our table and tried to figure out if it was a candle stand. Many of the courses had sauces. Marta was constantly pulling the scarf back and then putting it back on as soon as she was done putting down her fork. When the third course with a red sauce came around, Marta got concerned and immediately took the scarf off. Elena looked at her with a frown.

Inaki teased my mom, "You ate so much bread. We could have bought it from the local bread shop! How will you eat what the chef made?!" When a particularly pretty course came out, we asked our server to take a picture of us to remind us of this wonderful time. Most of the food had local ingredients. Local fish, local vegetables, local meat. I was thinking, that's good for the planet. We are reducing our carbon footprint. The food was healthy, but the company was even better. We were learning so much about Basque culture.

The conversation was light and we were relaxed. My dad raised his glass: "To friends for life and to a new running habit, only because Inaki shows up at our door at six a.m. daily!"

I added, "And to swimming in the ocean every day, because Elena and Inaki swam with me." Everyone raised their glass and our laughter tinkled.

Finally, the pigeon arrived. I asked my dad for some, but instead my mom passed me her plate with a look of relief and said, "Thank you, Siyona!" There was a bright red sauce and a piece of grilled meat with dark lines across it. Marta gulped down that course even though she had also had a lot of bread like my mom. I noticed that the scarf was on the chair now.

It was time for dessert! First they served cold, cut-up strawberries in wine glasses. Then with steel sprayers they added dollops of steaming whipped cream. "Was it just for show?" we wondered as nobody had expected that the whipped cream would be hot. My taste buds were confused by the contrast between the cold sweet strawberries and the hot cream, and I kept eating spoon after spoon to clear the confusion. I decided that the taste was like sweet snow melting away. Then I got a huge slice of apple pie with cream. Everybody except my mom dug into their dessert. The curved slices of baked apples with cinnamon and sugar were melting in my mouth. I finished my mom's chocolate cake. We all ordered chamomile tea. I sipped water to stay awake. The tea was served to us in our own little glass pots filled with steaming clear yellow liquid. The tea warmed me up inside and Marta leaned back in her chair sipping the tea slowly.

Our tummies were bursting and our hearts were cheerful. Marta carefully handed Elena her scarf back. Then she noticed something. "What's that?" she asked Elena.

"Oh", Elena said softly, her cheeks turning red, "I spilled some sauce on myself in the third course," as she tried to hide the red stains on her white shirt. We all worried that our long and loud guffaws would make us spill the food we had just had. Luckily for Marta, Elena's scarf was clean and healthy!

Two Poems

By Marjane Searl, 8
Indiana

Crickets

I turn and hear them
Soft, quiet, chirping voices
Speaking by music

Sunset

Warm, golden yellow
Against a vivid blue sky
Topped with clouds of pink

The day is over,
Yet a whispering on my mind
Gets me to calm down

Veins (iPhone 8)
Madeline Male, 14
Kansas

Spring Will Revive

By Hana Shqairat, 13
Palestine

The sun crawls its way past the horizon.
Snow dissolves into the abyss beneath the soil,
Clouds gather upon tradition.
All that lives droils.

Suddenly floral colors are slung across the sky,
Humid winds make their way
Past the joyful birds soaring high.
The leaves begin to sing and sway.

They all sing in harmony,
What a beautiful melody they make.
Their voices align perfectly,
Soothing all the aches.

The fruits ripen and come alive,
The hills sprout with a new cover.
Animals and insects strive,
The colors of life uncover.

Spring has arrived.
Along with its grace to heal.
Spring will revive,
And the world will kneel.

Highlight from Stonesoup.com

The Life of a Guinea Pig
Nova Macknik-Conde, 11

This fiction story is inspired by real events from the lives of my two guinea pigs, Oreo and Snickerdoodle, who were rescued from Prospect Park in Brooklyn, New York, in late 2021.

Oreo sniffled. His human family had taken him and his brother, Snickerdoodle, here to die. Oreo didn't really know where "here" was, but it was probably something like the wilderness. It was late fall, and soon he and Snickerdoodle would freeze to death in a cold, lonely place, with no food, no water, no shelter, no nothing. The last thing Oreo saw before his family took him away was a small brown puppy yapping at them. Oreo could only speculate, but he suspected that the puppy was to be their replacement. It was a terrible day to be a small, fragile, soon-to-be-preyed-upon guinea pig.

Because Snickerdoodle was brown, he could camouflage a bit better with the forest around them, but noooo, he just had to have their only hiding place, which wasn't even really a hiding place, just a tiny twig that didn't even cover a square inch of either of their bodies. Oreo was black and white, the exact opposite of their surroundings, so if a hawk or another predator came, he would be eaten immediately. Oreo started to cry. But then, a mysterious guinea pig appeared out of nowhere. It looked almost exactly like Oreo.

"Don't be scared!" the new guinea pig oinked.

"*Ahhhhh!*" Oreo screamed.

"Oh, come on, I *just* told you—you know what, never mind. Don't be sad that your humans abandoned you here, because I'm you from the future! Everything will be okay! You'll get rescued by a kind human, who will take you to your forever family!" Future-Oreo oinked happily, jumping for joy.

"But what about Snickerdoodle?" Oreo asked.

"Yeah, what about me?" Snickerdoodle whimpered.

"Oh, don't worry! They'll take Snickerdoodle too!" Future-Oreo said. "Bye! Don't forget what I said!" He oinked as he faded away.

You can read the rest of Nova's piece at https://stonesoup.com/post/stone-soup-monthly-flash-contest-winners-roll/.

About the Flash Contests
Stone Soup holds a flash contest during the first week of every month. The month's first Weekly Creativity prompt provides the contest challenge. Submissions are due by midnight on Sunday of the same week. Up to five winners are chosen for publication on our blog. The winners, along with up to five honorable mentions, are announced in the following Saturday newsletter. Find all the details at Stonesoup.com/post/stone-soup-monthly-flash-contest-winners-roll/.

Honor Roll

Welcome to the Stone Soup Honor Roll. Every month, we receive submissions from hundreds of kids from around the world. Unfortunately, we don't have space to publish all the great work we receive. We want to commend some of these talented writers and artists and encourage them to keep creating.

Printed in the USA
CPSIA information can be obtained
at www.ICGtesting.com
JSHW012028170224
57561JS00001B/1